CW01023848

SEMIOTEXT(E) INTERVENTION SERIES

© 2010 by Semiotext(e)
Originally published in *Recherches* n°12 *Trois milliards de pervers: grande encyclopédie des homosexualités* in March 1973.

Published by Semiotext(e)
2007 Wilshire Blvd., Suite 427, Los Angeles, CA 90057
www.semiotexte.com

Thanks to Alessandro Avellis, William E. Jones, and Erik Morse.

Design: Hedi El Kholti

ISBN: 978-1-58435-081-1
Distributed by The MIT Press, Cambridge, Mass.
and London, England
Printed in the United States of America

Guy Hocquenghem

The Screwball Asses

Translated by Noura Wedell

semiotext(e)
intervention
series □ 3

1 *

My God! What game are they playing? Come on, this is pure rubbish!

— Samuel Beckett

Let me start with the admission that what follows is exclusively addressed to those individuals with whom I cannot make love. For everyone else, the festivity of bodies transforms speech into a servant of the body, nothing else. It is not useless to specify this: we only speak of sex in front of people with whom it does not take place or who likewise admit to having no desire for us. The dichotomy between making love and speaking love does not come from me. On the contrary, I abhor it.

----

* This essay was originally published in the March 72 issue of *Recherches*, "Three Billion Perverts: An Encyclopedia of Homo-sexualities." The issue was seized, and Félix Guattari, as the publications director, was fined 600 francs for affronting public decency. No. 12 of *Recherches* was judged to constitute a "detailed display of turpitude and sexual deviation," the "libidinous exhibition of a minority of perverts." All copies of the issue were ordered to be destroyed.

May I posit that once desire shall have incorporated *non-desire* (or so-called non-desire), the revolution shall lose its object? For now, to speak of non-desire is absolute proof of its existence. And attempting to define the obstacles to desire will amplify them as well. An absurd enterprise, I admit, and even more absurd when it passes from speech into writing.

Most everyone agrees that the refusal of desire is sovereign: "*I don't want to, that's all!*" A white-collar bourgeois or an immigrant worker will tell you the same thing. And the left-wing student will repeat it even louder, for he has made desire sacred intellectually. As for me, when I hear someone express non-desire, I hear something behind it that could be: "*Don't insist! Capitalism has inscribed this refusal in my body.*"

I feel the need to write, rather than continue to speak about this issue, precisely because it has become impossible to speak of, even between people who share the same form of desire. This impossibility is even more severe when it affects the particular kind of homosexuality I wish to speak of: homosexuality that considers itself revolutionary, that in turn loses sight of the revolution, or falls prey to its pure theory, and that I will call *screwball homosexuality* (for fun).

Let me start from two recent anecdotes I was involved in, and which triggered my transition to a written explanation. Here is the first. Several homosexuals decide to get together in front of a tape recorder to discuss a book written by one of them called *Homosexual Desire*. These homosexuals communicate through their intellectual bonds and their shared political past rather than through their bodies; most of them have taken part in the constitution of the *Homosexual Front of Revolutionary Action* (FHAR),** and can be considered quasi-professionals in the liberation of homosexual desire. Suddenly, as if an amateur has slipped into their midst, someone says: "*It seems to me that we cannot speak about this book without first addressing the homosexual desire that exists between us and knowing how it circulates, or does not circulate, in this room.*" The most stupefying atmosphere of repression of speech and self-censorship immediately settles in. During the next three hours it becomes just as impossible to speak as it would be to have an erection: a situation of prohibited desire, in the midst of what we might call militants of desire, none of whom, may I add, have a body that is corrupted by nature or by age.

The second story unfolds at the École des Beaux-Arts in Paris. An open meeting is held in a lecture hall there, each Thursday at eight p.m., where homosexuals come to the FHAR to find an outlet for their desire for political struggle and sex. Let me make it

---

** We shall keep the French acronym, FHAR, Front homosexuel d'action révolutionnaire, in the rest of the text. (Translator's note.)

clear that no one, except for themselves, in any way thwarts their verbal, sentimental or bodily effusions. As I leave the meeting, a boy takes me by the arm and leads me towards an obscure passageway.

I enter into a dark, humid hovel where we wade in puddles of water and urine: the toilets of the Beaux-Arts. Half a dozen bodies, anonymous in the dim light, are enlaced there in what complex circuitries one cannot immediately decipher. I feel burdened by the enforced blindness, the acrid smell of piss chokes me and I recoil, feeling guilty immediately. The boy at my side murmurs in my ear: "*What? Are you ashamed?*" He might just as well have said: "*Are you ashamed, comrade?*"

Well, yes, I was ashamed. But I was ashamed of my shame. It is as if homosexual desire could only be inscribed where repression has inscribed it. I know how many queers only have toilets in which to touch each other. It depresses me that those who have decided to come out of hiding continue to project their excitement in the miserable places that the system condescends to allow them and where the police provoke them. Toilet spasms are like banking transactions: a flow of cum running in the shadows, as disincarnate as money, checks of cum behind the grate of a bank teller window.

I suddenly turn fascist and want to chase the queers from their tearoom with a whip. I want to throw them out of this cell where they can only revel in darkness. Strange paradox: they can desire almost any body with a dick and an ass (I wish I could), on the condition that it all happens in the shadows, that they fuck without knowing each other, that only machinic organs be involved.

Put the same people in a lit room, as we have just seen, or in a tranquil prairie (not to mention a public park), and they start talking to escape desire, or they look askance at one another, eyeing the only body with which they would like to be alone. The desiring machine produces crepuscular orgies or couples that close in under the light, and then shut off the electricity.

I could tell a third story. But its protagonists have taken it upon themselves to recount it in a text published here entitled "Arabs and Us." Very rarely have the twists of homosexual desire been exposed with such stupefying honesty by those who experience them, and anyone who has read the text has been plagued by intense, almost nauseating, doubt. A majority of readers will probably escape such feelings by filing the text away as pathological. The text, however, does not incriminate its own admissions, but those that remain untold, by which we mean the well-heeled forms of homosexual (or simply sexual) activity of those who experience, upon reading it, the slightest hint of nausea.

Such perversions are not mine, as I am certainly more bourgeois, yet they push me to question why I disdain the practices they describe and the spirit of such practices. I can't get out of this by saying it points to pure sexual misery where joy and true sharing are absent. I know only too well that joy is rare and that it is almost always the result of period privilege (certain primitives), privilege of age (certain children) or class (certain marginal bourgeois).

I have been privileged to encounter many dicks, not only Arab ones, many Arabs, and not only their dicks, but this does not give me the right to criticize or to reject a sexual structure that avowedly attains its highest pleasure only with Arabs and only with their dicks. The boys speaking in "Arabs and Us" do not declare their obsessions to be gospel; on the contrary, they insidiously imply that whoever condemns them can only do so in the name of some gospel or another.

What does the text say? The scene is Paris, but the background is the paradise of the Moroccan countryside, uncontaminated as yet by urban capitalist relations and where a subsistence economy subsists. The myth of the primitive operates in full force, ejaculation returns to precocious and brutal ingenuity, and one could easily become an Arab there oneself. But return to Paris is inevitable, and there, Arabs are no longer admirable Arcadian shepherds but industrial sub-proletarians. And that is where things get complicated. It is out of the question to open a whorehouse for Arabs in which we would be the whores, as it was in Marrakech. There is no escaping economics. Everything reverts to spectacle and exploitation. In this gigantic spectacle, the bourgeoisie directs the spectacle of the proletariat, but it is the proletariat who produces the bourgeoisie and its particularisms.

What the young gay man says to the Arab is still an avowal of guilt: "*The bourgeoisie exploits you, my father exploits you, so fuck me!*" And he might add: "*Doing this in my country, under the Clichy Bridge, is sordid; but in your country, in the bushes of Essaouira, it's so wonderful!*" Class struggle, class masochism, what hides beneath this artificial appropriation of the primitive?

In "Arabs and Us," some homosexual boys explain to us that their desire is looking for the primitive and the oppressed. But what they are looking for, instead, is someone that is the least capable of exerting power over them, and yet this social victim is the most male chauvinist of all. We might even say that bodies with a phallus but no penis are drawn towards bodies which have a penis without a phallus. What an extraordinary desire, not only does it satisfy itself, it commits a political act as an alibi: *I get fucked in the ass by the people my father and grandfather have fucked in the colonial wars, before doing so in their factories.* But such an equation is absolutely false: *I lend my ass for fifteen minutes to someone that the bourgeoisie has mythically sodomized its entire life, to the point of perfecting in him the male pride that was already instilled by Islam.*

Such an attitude might perhaps stand a chance of disrupting the mechanism of established roles if the European shouted at the Arab: "*Your virility is insolent! I love it!*" and if the Arab responded: "*So, you recognize I am a beautiful male! You can sodomize me now!*" That particular Arab would then escape his archetypical socio-sexual category. But it is already a rare occurrence to encounter an Arab who accepts to play the sodomized on the condition of being the active sodomite in the end. What is nonexistent, in "Arabs and Us," is the Arab who agrees to sodomize only if he is then sodomized in turn. There is reason for this: the latter would be Westernized, he would produce meaning instead of producing such animality as coded by Mohammed or Coca-Cola, and would no longer interest those queers who run after Arabs and who proclaim it in their confession.

If we read this confession a couple of times, without hostile *a prioris*, we discover that it contains a certain number of postulates. First, as we have seen, desire is cut off from the slightest revolutionary project: if an Arab has begun his sexual revolution, he is excluded from sex. Roles are not broken but granted. And let us add, so that there can be no misunderstanding on our part, racism must be enacted sexually: the sexuality of the queers speaking to us in this text demands racism as a particular form of exogamy; although, we cannot imagine how this racism might finally be wiped out.

Secondly, pleasure is radically separated from the confrontation of people, from all the Vaselines of psychology, in short, from all communication other than organic penetration. The homosexuals who concern us here segregate pleasure and communication. One of them proclaims the following sentence before a microphone, which is then communicated to us in writing: "*Communication is a fucking bore!*" The only remaining power relation is the muscular relation. So here we have the erection alone in its cage, a machine that does not believe it is human, nothing but pure machine. Love with a big "F" has assassinated love with a big "L," thank God.

In the end, what have Arabs become in this story where a thrust of the dick will never abolish chance? They are a collection of dildos, and we must not forget that a collector is always somehow a bourgeois. Turning his back to this pack of utensils and opening his ass to them, the Arab chaser queer dreams of being killed by a dick that obliterates his own, by an *ivory dick*, as he says, a primitive gadget that will transform him, in phantasm, into a hole without a dick, a dramatized woman, and that will deliver divine death to him.

If I now admit that such extreme behavior bewilders me and that perhaps I dream of it, my analysis will have been too critical to be believed. But the tape player that tells the story of "Arabs and Us" keeps turning in my head, and I hear a sentence repeat like a broken record. One of the boys keeps saying: "*There must be no dupes! I don't want there to be dupes! There are no dupes! There are no dupes! There are no dupes!*" And yet, he and his comrades propose a form of intellectuality that consumes primitive virility and cultivates phallocracy, all the while imposing its cultural law. And everyone is duped.

But this confession is exemplary nonetheless. Not all homosexuals experience such adventures, which they believe to be dangerous, and even these confessions make them cringe. Those who live them and dare tell about it at least do so fully. The bourgeoisie did not leave us many pathways to homosexuality; there is just one, all others lead to flight or masquerade. The text "Arabs and Us" gives an excellent picture of that path. Those who speak there are dupes but certainly not liars. Rather, the other queers are the liars or actors, who play either the comedy of the bourgeoisie or the comedy of the revolution.

2

It is good for a man not to touch a woman.
— Saint Paul

We queers have things to say and we have said them to those who defend themselves against their own homosexuality. But there are also things to say to those who glorify their homosexuality as being so particular and irreplaceable, and they are not the same things. As a dick always carries back some shit, because we are always depositing cum in shit or leaving some shit on the dick coming out of us, we are the stinkballs of the social game. Sodomized, we are the only ones to shit backwards. But being the least proper does not imply that we are the least propertied; being the most dissolute does not mean we are the most competitive; being the most machinic in no way lead to us to being the least romantic; nor does being the most marginal entail being the least bourgeois.

Our lobster walk, head down, tail up, is nothing but a cliché of normalcy reversed. We program homosexuality just like a heterosexual imagines it can be experienced, the same way he would speak of it or fantasize it, with males on one side and females on the other: here the bears that desire a failed man instead of a woman, here the flaming queers that desire a bear.

As long as queers continue to speak of themselves in the feminine and to ask, "*What time is it?*" when they meet, they shall consolidate sexism. A taxi driver turns to face the two queens chitchatting behind him, and blurts out, annoyed: "*I hate women!*" What a miracle, he has been forced to admit his phallocratic nature, but everything returns to normal when the queens reply: "*Well then, we can find an arrangement, there is a big bed at home...*"

Little boys who have not been forced to be males are not afraid of role-playing during recess: "*Let's pretend I'm a girl!*" But as adults, we cannot be rid of our obsession with women by pretending to be one.

I regret sometimes not allowing the woman within me to express herself enough. If I play the queen, I feel that I will only unveil the masculine masks of women. To make ridicule more ridiculous, shame more shameful, to the point of creating a spectacle of them, albeit useful exorcism, is to do the same as the bourgeois who make themselves up in gray or the revolutionaries who make themselves up in red. There is woman within me, why would I add more? I'd rather lose myself between the man and the woman that inhabit me, just as I lose myself when I masturbate: the one with the whip and the one being whipped, the one who binds and the one bound, the one on top and the one on the bottom, I don't know, my masturbation is a balance with two scales that gets freaky.

Yes, we copy normal relations, we either occupy the place of the subject or that of the object, but we copy them in any case. Today's homosexual does not embody polymorphic desire: he moves univocally beneath an equivocal mask. His sexual objects have already been chosen by social or political machination, and they are always the same: either weaker or stronger, older or younger, more in love with him or he more in love with them, more bourgeois or more proletarian, primitive or intellectualized, *uber*-male or sub-male, black or white, Arab or Viking, top or bottom, and so forth. Politics has already done its underground work. If, to boot, consciousness gets involved in political struggle, then the heterosexual and exogamic tendencies of today's homosexuality will become a caricature, and we will see more and more cases where a dick can only make love to a head and a head to a dick.

The movement is complex. Those who only have power through the body, that is, through beauty or through a desirable body, could desire anyone if they were entirely in their body, as is often the case in the non-Westernized world. But often in the Western world having only bodily power brings frustration. And so desirable bodies dream of another power than that of the body, and their desire turns towards those with the power of speech. This is a difficult relationship, it scares them sometimes, and they sometimes prohibit it for themselves for fear of being marked, but it is their true cybernetics.

In the same way, those who have power through speech without having lost power through the body could desire anyone. But the West has instilled in us such a dichotomy between the body and speech that having power through speech will eventually make us suspect that we have lost the desirability of the body. And so *speech bodies* refuse to make love to other *speech bodies*, speech against speech in the tumble of bodies, for they are afraid of abdicating their power of speech in the fray. And their desire turns back to those who only possess the power of the body and whose body they can mark by speech, or by their muted speech, or whose phallus can interrupt their own speech. Such *speech bodies* cannot speak while making love, and they even close their eyes to come in the dark, as do four French women out of five according to the recent Simon report.

The tense homosexuality of dissenting gays consists in fucking those who share the same sex, of course, but not twin languages or silences, and who, therefore, do not belong to the same origin, history, or lineage. Such homosexuality runs away from resemblance of mind and finds it necessary to construct its sexual objects within another race, class, culture, intellectual framework, objects that are, quite simply, of another age. These sexual objects must not correspond to them in thought, and it would be most difficult to share a life with them. This is a form of the prohibition against fraternal incest.

When we say that all social activity corresponds to the sublimation of homosexual interests for the public good, one must also add that this applies to gays, regardless of how comic the consequences seem. We play rugby, we play war, we play at free capitalist competition and political activism, but those who play at revolutionary homosexuality together are very careful not to sleep together, between comrades and friends: it just isn't the thing to do, you can't mix apples and oranges. The prohibition of fraternal incest is latent in homosexuality. It becomes imperial once political activism or anti political activism is involved. The political-desiring normative inclination of our caste has turned this very homosexuality into exogamy between brothers.

3

With the bath water
Throw yourself out
But not the baby.
— Mao Tse-Tung

Five years ago, one could not speak of homosexuality without mentioning the rest. Today, we cannot speak of the rest without mentioning homosexuality. No human being is innocent of it, nor can anyone speak of it objectively, outside of his or her desire or counter-desire.

Our homosexuality has been structured on a threat, and psychiatrists have made us believe that this threat arises from a paranoid anxiety of persecution. Never have cause and consequence been better reversed. It is on the contrary the social echo of what our desire threatened in repressed homosexuals that made us into what we are. And as one man we fell into the trap of becoming the persecuted.

Not only does the social body accuse me of a desire that it refuses in terror, but it also accuses me of becoming paranoid about it. Yet where is the desire for persecution stronger, in the accuser or in the persecuted? The persecution of homosexuality has its source in a homosexual desire. Whether they are passionate or scientific, all attitudes towards homosexuality are homosexual attitudes. When repression *pursues* a desire, it does so according to all acceptations of the term: it is obsessed about it, it tries to attain it, it runs for it and always lags behind, and it determines it as its goal.

But really, we are not the ones that homosexuality sends into a panic or sickens! It is heterosexual society that is continually panicked at the idea of seeing its homosexuality appear, against which its entire edifice is built. We have always been told that civilization was born of exogamy. Yet civilization exhibits so much sadism and terrified heterosexuality that we might start finding other basic components to it than simply the prohibition against incest: masochism and homosexuality, for example. Our entire psychological and economic organization is nothing but a masochistic and homosexual adventure, experienced without and against sex.

It is strange that the very presence of an avowed homosexual in a small group will induce any man to take on the paradoxical behavior of having to deny his homosexuality, to attack homosexuality and even to lash out against the homosexual in question, all the while acting as if this denial or attack were the most subtle of seductive techniques. This is called the *desire-fear* of being raped by a man, and when the contradiction grows too strong, this movement falls back upon the desire to rape a man.

We would be beating a dead horse by saying that psychoanalysis trumpets the existence of homosexuality everywhere. Unfortunately, it does not stop there: it immediately establishes that this homosexual libido, in which everyone participates, must be sublimated by sentiments, friendship and socioeconomic activity. The Oedipal prohibition enables family. The anal prohibition allows for salary, profit, and work. The homosexual prohibition enables and organizes all social sentiments concerning the cell, the group, the tribe, the company, the union, and the homeland.

Let us propose an amusing hypothesis: if, by some aberration, education were entrusted to homosexuals that were not missionaries of homosexuality, as were the Greek preceptors of Antiquity, the paranoia towards homosexuality would disappear and the very nature of homosexual desire would metamorphose by escaping guilt. (We are not at this juncture, however. The majority of homosexuals do not desire such a thing, for their bad conscience gives them a sense of equilibrium, and has even become, for some, the very basis of their security.)

While school and family made our homosexuality shameful, those institutions also made us as sick and policing as they were. The repression of homosexuality is riveted to the desire it is chasing, for this desire haunts it; thus, homosexuals can only construct themselves a morbid, that is to say, bourgeois universe. Repression is a cat without a smile in the heterosexual streets, and a smile without a cat in homosexual minds.

Almost all homosexual behavior is bourgeois, and this is not meant in the moral sense in which workerism denounces a class spirit or bourgeois stigmata. It is meant in the sense that homosexual desire is mechanically recited rather than invented. It is because this desire functions exclusively around sex, and not on the totality of the body. It is because it is not so indisputable that the anus ignores sexual difference, because it is not so certain that the reinvestment of the anus will weaken the great phallic signifier, since the desiring use of the anus calls for the phallus just as strongly as does the orthodox social usage of the vagina, even if it passes over shame.

Not only does the gap between desiring a hold on the phallus of others and fearing to lose one's own characterize the social game of the anti-homosexual bourgeoisie, but this gap also subsists in a more delirious form in homosexual practice, which remains competitive, even and especially when the anus is reinvested therein. The fact that one is also an anus does not defeat the menace weighing on the phallic existence of the queer, just as the voluntary disappearance of the anus neither justifies nor explains this menace in ladies' men.

In sum, reintroducing the anus can degrade the phallic signifier only if it reaches all society, and furthermore, only if anal penetration is performed in both directions, in couples considered to be the elementary component of study. However, we know that the heterosexual couple can only reach this stage by using accessories and fetishes.

Finally, we must also have the courage to recognize that homosexual desire is not only recited by heart, it is recited by a repression of the heart. And in the end, its apparatus of possession retains a molar structure, regardless of the seemingly fetishistic attachment to partial objects which continually resuscitates the phallus.

It is true that the homosexual anus contributes to the crisis of Oedipal civilization. Yet it does so in a complex and contradictory manner, by injecting so much normalcy into the circuit that we can neither postulate the radically revolutionary essence of homosexual desire, nor its sure-fire trajectory towards the indifferentiation of desire and the refusal of anthropomorphic sexuality.

Oh! How we wish, by freeing the human, that we could liberate the non-human! How we wish to transform not only the religion or politics of the human, but and above all, its anatomy! We know full well that no masculine being in the West can experiment his sexuality without demanding penetration, unless he is a monk, a schoolboy, or prepared to lose his virility. This is what capitalism has wanted, or revealed, to the point of caricature. It is also how capitalism maintains its grasp on us. And we cannot respond to this by begging for the sex of angels.

More often than not, we homosexuals are not abnormal; rather, we have failed normalcy. We are as codified by the bourgeoisie as the latter has sexually codified workers by making them failed bourgeois. Rather than being lovers in order to breathe, we are queer in order to escape asphyxia. Rather than pretending to be virtuous, we pretend to be dissolute. And if the self-management of desire turned out to be virtue, we would refuse it, already intimating discipline and obligation there. As long as we are not burned at the stake or locked up in asylums, we continue to flounder in the ghettoes of nightclubs, public restrooms and sidelong glances, as if that misery had become the habit of our happiness. And so, with the help of the state, do we build our own prison.

4

Speak to my ass. My head is sick.
— Southern French Proverb

Like the women's liberation movement that inspired
it, the revolutionary homosexual platform emerged
with Leftism and traumatized it to the point of con-
tributing to its debacle. But while they fissured
Leftism by revealing its phallocentric morphology and
its censure of marginal sexualities (and of sexuality in
general), these autonomous movements, despite their
refusal of hierarchy, continued and continue to repli-
cate the conditioned reflexes of the political sector
that produced them: logomachy, the replacement of
desire by the mythology of struggle, the use of charm
diverted to public discourse and considered to be a
nuptial parade and an accession to power.

Therefore, early on in the FHAR's orbit we
encountered paranoia, mania and, above all, the
cruel internal aggressiveness that we had picked up
in the trashcans of Leftism. We might have hoped
that homosexuality could tear classic activism away

from non-desire, inject it with a dose of epicurism and create a true celebration of our colluding desires, but that was without taking the bad conscience of homosexuals into account. We must admit that the wildfire was short-lived.

As a masculine sect that was rapidly deserted by the lesbians because of its phallic surcharge, the FHAR could never resolve the contradiction of having to fight against virility with virility, understood as an internal need or latent state, as its only weapon. Here, we rebuilt the Leftist theater. There, we rebuilt the carnival of stars to assemble the next barricades in evening gowns. Theory for the sake of theory collided with madness for the sake of madness, and they both tried to reconcile themselves in the imperialism of youth and beauty. For, just as collectibles are deemed beautiful when old, bodies desired only as objects are only deemed beautiful when young.

Today, after having weathered the storms of exclusions, having undergone the virile or falsely feminine game of power rivalries and suffered either centrifugal or suicidal behavior towards the movement, the FHAR survives in the form of a reassuring protoplasm or a uterine chamber. We flirt or befriend people there, but never both at once. We show each other our great ancestors. Unless we are one of those, our existence depends upon being desirable. On the other hand, if we are the ones that desire, then we shrink to an ectoplasmic state as if we were cruising a gay club. It is not the place for pleasure to be had in public. Leftism has passed through, and Leftism dries up whatever it touches.

Whatever comes from Leftism will remain permeated by terrorism and factionalism. For fear of not following the tacit scripture or counter-scripture that is supposed to unite us, in that environment we always feel as if we were the students or the professors of those who have spoken last, even if this is against our will. We could even say that the desire to deconstruct all relations of power, the uninterrupted lookout for relations of power, creates an additional, hallucinatory power relation.

Of course, within the FHAR, there are and have been attempts made to reject this whole mechanism of the persecuted and the persecutor, but the crisis has not been resolved. Today, the collective body of revolutionary queers lies emptied, lifeless and useless; and this happened faster to the FHAR than to any other leftist group.

I do not call this a catastrophe. One bubble bursts. Other bubbles reach the surface. It is a good thing that assemblages do not turn into institutions. Better to start by pushing the real divisions of individuals to their maximum instead of collecting them in unions or corporations that contain but a minimal portion of true community. Yet I do wonder when we will leave behind savagery. And by savagery I do not mean nudity, primitiveness or spontaneity (that Leftists have transformed into totally artificial nudism, primitivism and spontaneism), but *malevolence*, if it must be named.

The comic kindness of the bourgeois has made us dramatically mean. We have learned from political analysis that non-violence is humanist devilry, that courtesy is a class heritage and a deceptive pretense, that non-conflictual speech is a salon masquerade. We took stock of the consequences a bit too fast. In order to keep a steadfast watch on the contradictions and hypocrisies of others (who do the same to us), we established a reciprocal mechanism of removal, attorney's work through which the revolution is supposed to grant us power of attorney and to speak for each of us. The revolution remains, but we are no longer there. So that when our necessary aggressiveness bursts with these internal tears, it unfortunately does not correspond to its floating sources.

In the Revolutionary Men's Club there are no *nice members*. In most of my comrades (those that I still dare call by that name), sadism and masochism appear through an antiquated political axiomatic, and not through the skin. The whip flashes without interruption, but the body never receives nor gives a lash. It is almost completely out of bounds in these men who speak of disposing freely of bodies. It begins with their eyes, their ears, their mouth and their hands, for they do not know how to look, hear or taste and they do not dare touch.

This situation has reached the point where the strangeness and phantasmagorical anomaly of daily life that capitalism has created is fought against even before it is perceived. Since they know that everything is misery, exploitation and political trickery, and since they have established that everything must be systematically criticized, they have completely forgotten the pleasure of observing their surroundings. Even the simple faculty of perception, namely what the bourgeois have lost, is considered a dishonorable sign of bourgeois privilege. Extensive use of the senses is perceived as an insult to the proletarians, whose bodies have been stolen by capitalism just as capitalism has dissolved the bodies of the bourgeois. Physical sensibility to the planet and the play of receptive organs would appear to conceal an enemy of the revolution or some diabolical form of power.

Of course, the proletariat is prevented from playing and from experiencing pleasure. But is it only through solidarity that the students at the heart of Leftism prevent themselves from doing so, or only play cops and robbers? What kind of anxiety separates these men from their bodies, men who scream of sex all day long? Are all games contaminated because their fathers could only play the stock market, the races, or playing house? Is it because all our society's games are competitive that we cannot imagine any that are not?

We play with great reluctance, even where there are no winners or losers to the game. Many people think of the revolution as a series of struggles, defeats and victories. I see it rather as a canvas, spreading, in movement, with a loose weave. Is it too serious an affair to be placed in the hands of players? Let us not forget that one of the rules of the ridiculous game of capitalism is to stop the revolution from being a game, to make sure that it never grows opposed to docile reality, that it never goes against obeying this so-called reality.

Not only have Leftists blocked off their senses, they have also constructed a language in which half the words are suspect, or tainted because they have been colonized, swindled of their meaning either by religion, by the bourgeoisie, or by Marxist or Freudian ideologies. Proof through etymology is passé. A word leaks out and we cover our mouth in shame under a barrage of cries and slander.

If you've got nerve, try pronouncing the words fraternity or benevolence in front of a Leftist assembly. Must we deduce from this impossibility that such things are not even remotely possible? Well, Leftists seem to have decided upon it. They have given themselves over to the studious exercise of animosity; they are engaged in deriding everything and anyone, regardless of whether they are present or absent, friend or foe. Theirs is not a system for progressing through contradiction, or for passing from one contradiction to another, but for wallowing in it. What is at issue is not to understand the other but to keep watch over him and be ready to smack his fingers if ever he reaches out.

In such conditions, speaking is stepping out on the razor's edge, tottering between self-censorship and guilt, afraid of being interrupted or attacked. The strangest thing is that such long lasting objections and reprimands function just as well inversed, so that they interrupt or impose speaking, silence becomes taboo, it is never experienced as joyful, and everyone conspires to lose his or her defenses it in.

Consequently, any interruption of displeasure is perceived as coming from the other and desired by that other. What we call *attention* is not attentiveness and openness to the other, it is being aware of the other as dangerous, like a car surging behind us in rapid traffic. In this way, the field of prohibitions grows much larger than it is in the bourgeois universe, and the field of receptiveness becomes just about as cramped.

If you try to explain this, you will be confronted with a surge of critiques and projections. A dry sirocco of interpretations will swell up, pertaining only to the words pronounced, as if the one pronouncing them did not exist. In this way, everyone's taboos are protected behind a more or less skilled network of justification, as if all possible situations were built on stratagems.

And yet, despite the disgust of daddy's humanism, and, as if some stench of democratic fat lingered on, the tacit assumption remains that no one shall be excluded. Everyone can speak to everyone, but from within a dictatorial language, which means that no one speaks to anyone, or, in fact, that only codes do.

In this web of discourses, we will certainly not allow ourselves to cry or to laugh until we cry and then forget why we did so. Pouring out your feeling is not serious, it is rather discrediting. Come on! A Leftist is neither a player, nor a *jouisseur*; he just drills people, regardless of whether he wants to liberate homosexuality or the proletariat. Never overwhelmed, the Leftist just saves himself for next time.

The Leftist does not have time on his side. He's always in a rush. He produces speed everywhere so as to force you into hysterics or into a daze. But it's not the kind of speed that propels you far away so that you find yourself stunned at having covered so much ground, stunned by the change of perspective and of thinking. Instead, it's the haste of the monkey scratching at the same spot till a sore develops. That kind of animal will go on in public monologue to no end, rambling about the difficulty of being together; he will change the world without touching himself and keep running after a certain month of May; he will continue to live his sexuality divorced from thought, and thoughtlessly if possible, in obscure situations where identity and groundwork are not at risk and desire is not exposed.

Terrorists the lot of them! Terrorists of theoretical discourse, terrorists of a perfectly channeled delirium, terrorists of nihilistic scorn, it's all the same: they answer oppression in the terms of oppression. What I am writing here does not escape the virus and will inevitably follow the same path. Either my reflections will exert terrorism in turn, and bring forth inhibitions. Or they will be quickly denied and carefully covered under an interpretation meant to rein them back into the domain of what is tolerable and questionable. Or no one will even listen.

Because the gears of Leftism have fallen in ruins. And yet the machine keeps running, like a record stuck on the same groove. Like a ghost. Like a blind dog taking himself for a guide dog.

5

What is done out of love is religious, not moral.
— Nietzsche

The psychiatrist André Morali-Daninos has written: "*If homosexuality were to receive the slightest, even theoretical semblance of approval, if it were, even partially, allowed to leave the framework of pathology, the heterosexual couple and the family that constitute the base of the Western civilization that we inhabit would rapidly be abolished.*" Oh, dearest, bravest, most dear and precious man! No other fragment of typical bourgeois discourse on homosexuality has had greater impact on gays at the beginning of their struggle. No sentence could have justified them more.

But things have changed. Early imperatives have disappeared. Revolutionary homosexuals no longer need to declare or define themselves—in the face of the liberal bourgeois or of their Leftist brothers—by borrowing their language or by confronting the so-called scientific objectivity of the one or the other.

We realize now that inverting the psychiatrist's phrase is dangerous. Its inverted postulate is as follows: "*If heterosexuality were to receive the slightest, even theoretical semblance of approval from homosexuals, if it were, even partially, allowed to leave the framework of phallocracy and of the reproduction of the species, the homosexual couple as a symbol of revolt and of the refusal of normalcy, at the base of our condition and our fight, would rapidly be abolished.*"

We must be wary of Stalinist types of reasoning: it is not by turning them upside down that things will change. And yet many gays among us did not hesitate a moment. For them, the revolution consisted in freeing and making official those places reserved for homosexual desire. It meant creating thousands of tearooms and millions of gigolos reimbursed by social security, rather than starting the revolution by publicly announcing the object of your desire, and asking in public who desires you.

Clandestine practices create addictions. And from those addictions, complaints emerge, creating some sort of enforced normalcy. We are just starting to see how those screwball homosexuals have been able to escape perceiving signs of their own alienation in their speech, and where to locate the reactionary body armor they hide.

Persecuted desire starts to function based on a number, like counter-espionage. In gays, that number is complex. Their desire is abominably eccentric: the desire a man might have for another man does not necessarily resemble his dream that that masculine object be a woman, or the same dream applied to himself. For it is always the case that the image of woman will reintroduce itself into masculine homosexuality. Our homosexual desire is racked by contradictions as we superimpose monomaniacal practices onto its heterodoxy and eccentricity.

Yet certain theoreticians of revolutionary homosexuality are trying to make us homosexuals believe, in a pedagogical move to rid us of guilt, that we decode our flows of desire as much as possible. Saying this, they take our desire for revolution for the practical reality of our libidinal desire. But mostly, they undermine the fact that, even if we do decode those flows, it is only to recode them again immediately. For we are just as formalized in our social geometry as those who are normal, since we define ourselves in the resistance we oppose to them.

Such theoreticians also claim that our revolutionary emergence engages us towards the disappearance of objects and subjects. But we are just as bound as heterosexuals by the villainy of power relations. They tell us, and it is true, that bisexuality can only find its source in the universal acknowledgment of homosexuality in each one of us, yet they forget to add that our homosexuality has its imaginary and social source in the heterosexual regime.

Finally, the newest discovery of the neo-structuralists of homosexuality is to stigmatize soppy affectivity and the abject desire to be loved, both sentiments derived from humanistic values. At this point, their reasoning stops being magic and becomes a conjuring act, the body of the crime vanishes: we must simply forget that our obsessive defense against sentiments and against the couple represses the scariest and most unyielding sentimentality. All we have to do is watch our desire conquer and refuse to occupy a supposedly mine-ridden terrain to see that we are still false nomads, hypocritical henchmen of sedentary sexuality and nothing more than apprentice lovers.

If the desire to be loved is abject, we are its main repositories. I would like to be a gigolo offering myself to all. But when I meet a gigolo who dazzles me, who seduces with even more insolence than myself and with more of that desire to be desired, am I not just as scared of a trap as everyone else, just as scared as he is? Scared of the trap of being less desired than I myself desire, the trap that is called being in love.

This is where we should scramble the flows, de-desire, en-desire, switch the current, disrupt the machine. But instead, we turn off the power because we are scared of suffering or of being swindled. No discipline is more *sentimental* than the one that represses sentiments. And who knows, perhaps what is most abject in us comes from the pleasure of being loved, that is, the refusal of the desire to love?

We do not have children. We do not secrete that kind of surplus value. (It isn't simply our refusal of women that stops us from having children. It is the bourgeois law of adoption that will only entrust parentless children to bourgeois and heterosexual couples, duly recognized after investigation by the police. Not only do we not fertilize women, but our situation prohibits our transformation by those tiny barbarians.) We are thus the strongest remedy to the natalist pollution of the planet. If we were the only ones here, humanity would immediately cease: no one would be born, there would be no children or adolescents, and we would become peaceful nihilistic old men sodomizing one another.

Who likes to hold a younger body in his arms more than a queer? They are so dear to us, those bourgeois couples so mythically upholding the succession of generations, the transmission of capital, the sacrifice for offspring, and who provide us with godlike boys that we know shall become more and more homosexual in the debacle of moral values that we work so hard for!

Of course, some of us, myself included, would like the border between biology and psychology to crumble before the progress that the homosexual movements, and each homosexual's own search, have made. It would be nice not to have to recognize paternity or the anxiety of disappearance. If we think that we must simply proclaim the fact for it to occur, then we are falling prey to a magic trick bequeathed us by a moribund Leftism and camouflaged beneath political theorems.

The most absurd of these theorems is the proclamation of the death of love. Love is only dead in certain minds. This is not because it is bourgeois, but because its contamination, by the bourgeoisie, by property, by security, has rendered it inane.

We know what love signifies for those who shield themselves from the folly of making love through the poetic and reactionary wisdom they have placed in the word. As for us, we must rid it of that sentimental glue that socialist as well as capitalist culture has enjoined to smother raw emotion, anesthetize the sensory, render imagination banal and that has come to usurp their place. Because Order will always find defense and justification in such sentiments as it has previously injected in the people. In order to tear ourselves away from such archaic viscosity, Which we have been told since the Middle Ages is the human condition, love would have to mean nothing else but an effervescent *desire to desire*, that is, *the opposite of falling in love*.

Yet the tense and disunited sexual liberation army fights love and death with the same determination, since both terms point to the same desire to lose oneself. Love and death hate the self. When the self hates them as well, orgasm becomes spectral; it stops baying at the moon, it stops being religious and political to become a moral issue, a question of restraint, of precautions. And this isolation into twos, as we have seen, does not resist the general isolation of all.

Here I am speaking of death. And yet I know that the essential relation between death and speech fascinates thought, even though we cannot yet really think it. The aristocracy, the bourgeoisie and the proletariat of the West, allied for once, have never stopped concealing death. Whether it is a cadaver, one's own cadaver, or even the idea of dying, it is against death that we build barricades, as if we had to live longer than the revolution.

In everything that I have observed through the collective struggles in which I took part, I have never seen death considered as a political fact or event. On this point, philosophy and politics have moved over to let destiny speak, that blind old dodderer. Naively, I believe, to take up a well-known phrase, that if revolution must stop at the perfection of happiness, then dying must also become something joyful.

Strangely enough, whenever we propose an idea like this, it is immediately taken to be Christian or mystical. Strangely enough, whenever we speak of joy, professional revolutionaries only hear what churches or ideologies have put there. The concept of *jouissance* has recently been brought into the vocabulary of revolt, but not the concept of joy, as if Saint-Francis of Assisi or Ramakrishna were necessarily behind it. Marx does not speak about sex and Freud never speaks about love, unless he is describing a bourgeois and Oedipal mechanism. But when we shall have gotten rid of Christ, of Marx, of Freud, of *Star*

Magazine, of Tristan and Isolde and all the vocabulary they have branded, won't love, joy and death still exist?

What sets me apart from many of my companions on the road we have collectively taken, it seems to me, is not that age has left me with a greater number of scars. The bourgeois continually refer to this difference by the name of experience. They use it to justify their precepts and to force their children to follow their path. I really don't care about this issue of transmitting experience. My scars are my own, what they teach is only for me to know. Nor do I think that life with a partner, or the distortions of writing, have transformed me into an abnormal homosexual.

Perhaps what makes me different is a certain political idea of death, an idea finally torn away from metaphysics. Of course, it is extremely improbable that such an idea will appear to students and young militants, unless perhaps under the guise of suicidal romanticism. But neither do I find it in President Nixon's speeches, in Mao's writings, and it seems much too esoteric in the works of Doctor Freud.

Clearly, love and death are banned from the political discourse of the bourgeoisie as well as from the discourse of the preceptors of the sexual revolution. For the bourgeoisie and for the Communist Party, sex is family, and family must be love. It seems clear enough. For the autonomous sexual movements that call themselves revolutionary, and particularly for homosexuals, sex is desire, and desire is politics. But love, that is, the desire to desire, has been cast off, as if it were nothing but a superstructure built as a trompe l'oeil in the structure of desire. As for death, neither the bourgeois nor revolutionaries ever talk about it.

I wonder where my interest in love and death came from. I am probably referring to some old knowledge that existed prior to the bourgeoisie, which then channeled all desiring production towards strictly economic surplus value. We are touching here upon a territory that is so strongly irrigated with magic that the mechanism of thought of all social classes has turned to magical trickery in order to return it to its own logical domain.

Until now, the revolutionary project has treated love and war in approximately the same manner. Either it censors them, as do the warring brother descending from Marx, or it approaches them with the intention of rendering them dependent and subordinate to a phallic and Oedipal discourse, as in the case of the warring brothers descending from Freud. And the conscientious workers of Freudo-Marxism, the eternal dialectic trowel in hand, have rushed headlong into the great breach that *Anti-Oedipus* has opened between the two.

And all the while, everywhere around us, we stupidly continue to die of love, we continue to commit suicide because we fall prey to all that resists love, we continue to die (or sometimes to survive, but as if we were dead), because the abject desire to be loved runs idle.

6

To make Swiss cheese, you take a hole and you put some cheese around it.

— *Vermot Almanac*

If I say that the phantasmatic produces a large part of our reality, I cannot believe that it occupies it completely, and thus evade its coexistence and ill-known interferences with the biological. Yet all of our research is still terribly fragmented. In what follows, I take the responsibility of pushing the bio-physical and biochemical to the side. The social sphere, in any case, is nothing but a chaotic mix of phantasms which all stem socially from the unique model of heterosexuality, a model that has circulated an incredible number of clichés issuing from classical psychoanalysis.

It is assumed, for example, that homosexuality is narcissistic. But the heterosexual, naively searching in vain for his homologue in the other gender, is branded by narcissism as much as the homosexual, who searches for his opposite in the same gender, imprinted with the heterosexual model that he refuses to follow and yet mimics.

If we examine the limit case of the transvestite, we realize that he is more woman than women, since he desires to be a woman whereas a woman is subject to her gender. And since the only image of women is a masculine one, this man shall recite woman a thousand times better, without intermediaries, without any orders being transmitting to the other, once he has decided to apply that image to his own body, instead of to his mother, his sister or his wife. The transvestite is the most perfect image of the woman man desires and the image farthest removed from the woman whose existence man obstructs.

In the same way, the homosexual who dreams he is sodomized is clearly searching for a man; he assimilates himself to a woman who is looking for a man and phantasmatically responds much more to the notion of heterosexuality than to the notion of homosexuality. In order for him to be truly homosexual, he would have to become a lesbian, but only if he found himself faced with a woman who did not dream herself a man, or the schema would revert to heterosexuality. In the same way, the woman who dreams of herself as penetrating, with her castrated man's imaginary, would have to become a gay man in order to be homosexual, but only if she found herself before a man who did not dream himself a woman, or again the schema would revert to heterosexuality.

In sum, true homosexuality could only be a woman desiring a woman and a man desiring a man, without their imaginaries introducing any image of the other gender whatsoever. Or it could occur in the case of a man and a woman who would both be gay, or a man and a woman who would both be lesbians. These situations seem clearly impossible, for, in spite of himself, the homosexual is of his own gender as much as he is of the other gender that he dreams of and that always searches for its opposite. So that even homosexuality is repressed homosexuality since its imaginary is heterosexual.

The same reasoning would lead us to say that there could only be true heterosexuality in a man who desires a woman or in a woman who desires a man without their imaginaries ever introducing any image of the same gender. But that, however, is perfectly possible, and has even been realized by the imaginary of heterosexual society, since it has anesthetized any homosexual imaginary.

Therefore, instead of being first, primary, animal, somatic, our homosexuality is just a response to heterosexual practices and diktats. This means that it suffers from an indigestion of heterosexuality. On the one hand, since those dear normal people whom have brought us into this world have hidden their homosexual libido, nine homosexuals out of ten people chosen at random do not even consciously exist. (We know this well: in the human species not only is one man out of every two a woman, but half of the other man is also a woman. One man out of every two is a woman, and the other does not know that he is also gay.) We thus find ourselves in a crazy situation where homosexuality can only be heterosexual or not at all.

Since we are not homosexuals in any elementary way, it is time to stop proudly shouting our shame. "*You are homosexuals*" is what we should be shouting out to all, even if we must become hysterical in the process. And since it is established that there can be no real bisexuality without homosexuality first being experienced as such, our revolutionary activity could be to cause, by any means possible, the homosexuality of the silent majority to germinate beneath its anti-homosexual paranoia. If desire starts to circulate between men who usually connect to women, they will inevitably become more homosexual than we are, because woman will not be an unknown and ghostly body between them.

In the same way, we gays will have to experience a kind of homosexual homosexuality in which the other gender, once it is exiled, will finally stop reappearing on the stage of the theater of sodomy. If not, then we are still, or already, phantasmatically the heterosexuals that we refuse to be.

It is when I am masculine that I want to make love to a man. It is when I am feminine that I want to make love to a woman. That is the secret to all my masturbations (for I shall continue, even if all humanity desires me, to cheat on it with myself).

When a woman, and not a lesbian, shall make love to a woman without dreaming of the phallus or replacing it, when a man, and not a gay man, shall make love to a man without shakily dreaming of the vaginal hole and substituting an ass for it, then homosexuality shall have begun. From that minute on, homosexuality shall be able to melt into bisexuality, without deceit, without mistakes, without illusions. Once we have purged ourselves of the gender that we do not have and that we imitate, once we have purged ourselves of it with an instant of authentic homosexuality (that the body swears is not just an operative concept), then ambivalence will no longer be ambiguous.

Then we can be of one gender and dream ourselves of the other with the same consciousness, the same intensity and a simultaneity that allows for all possible connections: heterosexuality and homosexuality stop being each other's policing force. Orgasm, and the road to orgasm, are finally a joyous risk of death, as they were when the threat of death was perpetual. Sexuality stops terrifying the world but *arouses* it.

7

...maintain the perpetual immoral unhinging of the machine...

— Sade

Active, passive, old bullshit. For man to be virile, all women and gays must be passive. So goes the public rumor. But to be sodomized is only passive for those who, having never been sodomized, have never felt what effervescent anal *activity* is. Proof is that the man who is being fucked, finding himself between two men, cannot equally cum without exploding from such opposing phantasies. His *jouissance* must choose, and more often than not, it attributes greater importance and strength to the most prohibited and transgressive, the dick in his ass rather than the ass around his dick.

Both key and lock at the same time, this sodomite who is being fucked is in the best position to tear apart established roles, for sodomy is only subversive if it is reversible. If his body, with its two penises, could stop knowing whose they were, if they could cancel each other out, this extreme figure would paradoxically resemble that of two lesbians who connect without a male plug.

I hope I will be granted these phantasies and the utopia that goes with them. The fact remains that homosexuality can only escape heterosexuality by becoming a relation of weaknesses, of non-rivalry, or non-property, that is, by inverting male paranoia into schizophrenia. If reserve and human respect remain whole, as in transfixed, suffering and dignified lovers, if the purity of sentiments absorbs the shadows, then the homosexual is but half a rebel. Rigged with a mythical third sex, he continues to drone out virility, the tests of conquest, and an aching heart.

We should find out what the obstacles are to that *Pasionaria* movement which would enable gays to say, with their body rather than with words, "*All you need to do is desire me for me to desire you.*" Yes, I am dreaming aloud. In my dream, gays can be queens without running backwards towards big dicks. In my dream, they can hold a beautiful boy close, and that boy isn't necessarily the one to spread his cheeks. In my dream, they run neck and neck with desire without worrying that it stops at a single body to rest. In my dream, desire linkers on one body without restraining its unbridled desire for another.

The gays in my dream, my lovers, my friends, my enemies and myself, we can no longer distinguish desire from what is called love. And in my dream we can experience the same joys with women. For I cannot imagine the dissolution of normalcy without the so-called intersexual states becoming universal. I see no other way to get rid of the tyranny of virility, a tyranny, it should be said, that oppresses men just as much as it does women. To demand the recognition of homosexuality as it exists today, colonized by heterosexual imperialism, is simply reformism. It is not for us, it's for those good souls in *Arcadia*, at a birthday party, who invite the Police commissioner to the table of honor.

The queer is a traitor whose greatest fear is betraying normalcy. And once he has overcome that shame, he realizes by betraying normalcy, what he did in fact was bow to it. Our own, more Machiavellian game, could be to allow the repressed half of desire, whether homosexual or heterosexual, to gush forth from everyone. Man should allow himself to desire man as much as he desires woman. And in the same way, man should allow himself to desire woman just as much as he desires man.

Let us disorient flows so that man can desire in his body, himself first, and then man as much as woman, till he can no longer tell the difference between the two. This does not mean that we must reconcile the forms of sexuality that have been imposed by societal Oedipus. On the contrary, we must refuse that exclusive disjunction that, by means of sexual differentiation, has exhausted the body beneath the weight of gender and caused the proliferation of extra gender everywhere, as if genetics hadn't produced enough.

Genotype and phenotype carry enough weight as it is. What is the use of tagging on a historical gender, a psychological gender and a legal one? While it was repressing the polyvocity of desire, society was creating oversexed bodies that are now nothing but sexual organs. Perhaps the time has come to live our corporality rather than speak our sexuality.

Of course, we're not crazy enough to flood the phallocrats with female hormones. But there is a chance that the gradual disappearance of phallocracy, followed by a deep desire for intersexuality instigating a change in lifestyle, might very possibly, by the continual breakup of sexual roles, lead to biogenetic mutations in the long term. Although such a hypothesis might seem like science-fiction, it is spellbinding: it is a utopia in which our heterosexuality would no longer be molar or social, our homosexuality no longer personal and marginal, our transexuality no longer elementary and secret, since the three would connect in the same bodily place and be so melded together that we would no longer need several words to distinguish them.

Of course, this abstract state has never existed, nor will it ever exist, for it would signify the end of the sexual revolution. Getting there is not what matters. What matters is getting closer. If certain groups continue to believe they are stronger than sexual institutions, if they continue to announce that and to be in fact stronger, they will tear those institutions apart in themselves.

8

If we stopped distinguishing the sexes, who would notice what differentiates them?

— Milarepa

Why do we continue searching for the hidden sources of homosexuality, and devise guilty pathways for it, as if we necessarily had to wrench half of the world away from desire? Thought, by feeling mortal, has become the rival of nature, or has revolted against it. There is nothing else distinguishing humans from animals than this struggle against nature taking place under the guise of an alliance with it.

Man has become a counter-natural animal, and we have called that process the appearance of intelligence. As we rebel against our planet, our only option is to brand it with our filthy footprint, our moral calamity and our human pollution. Perhaps we will finally decide to derail the planet and desire it completely, its history and geography, its insects and hippopotamuses, its young and old, its males and females.

Homosexuality does not stem from any dirty little secret. The social mechanism repressing it is what generates guilt. There is a proportion of humans, oscillating between fifty and a hundred percent, that carries the desire for the same sex. Popular common sense, completely permeated by Judeo-Christian culture, refuses this obvious fact. And yet counter-culture sometimes unveils it in moments of lucidity, when it stops pretending to imitate nature, when it stops using nature, almost theologically, as an alibi.

There is no morality that does not claim to spring from the respect of nature, yet the foundations and the desire for morality are economic. (Let me remark that the most ferociously anti-abortionist of our ministers, whose stance supposedly arises out of a great respect for life, also presides over the production and distribution of the most killing machines, while his colleague in Public Health is brazen enough to declare, without fear of ridicule, that he finds some contradiction in seeing the same people campaign *against* the death penalty and *for* the massacre of innocent fetuses.)

Ants do not have abortions. Ants are not homosexual. Ants do not draft wills. Ants do not travel to the moon. Ants do not play football and do not play on Wall Street. Ants are natural. With the human machine, it's the opposite. We can read our condition most legibly in those areas that are the farthest removed from our conditioning, those zones between order and desire where the sting of injury is the greatest, and the callus covering the wound is most developed.

Homosexuality is not the result of a pallid (and so-called individual) childhood adventure; it is rather a capital point of conflict between society and the cultural nature of man. It is sufficient that one species move beyond the animal for the homosexual alternative to become inherent and grow to define it, even if this species defends itself from it ferociously by invoking the laws of nature. Nature, however, is not made of laws but of phenomena. Ignoring this obvious fact, we go searching for morals where there have never been any: in the animal world, whose unbearable cruelty we are very careful to silence beforehand. Ours is a society of sublimated homosexuality. This is the only way that we can speak of a homosexual conception of the world.

If the human being, and man in particular, claims he is heterosexual with such insistence, and he produces such a wealth of moral and metaphysical justifications for this claim, it is, of course, because he condemns and represses the homosexuality in himself and refuses to recognize that he is as drawn to his gender as he is to the other. Such concealment, by burying that desire, only increases and deforms it. On the contrary, when a small group chooses to publicly express its homosexuality against all social regulations, it does so by prohibiting heterosexuality and stamping it with the sign of damnation as the State imposed form of copulation. And thus, unrecognized, the homosexual entity becomes the source of two interdependent forms of racism which are nourished there. If, on the contrary, it were recognized and expressed by all, homosexuality would dissolve at the same time as heterosexuality, and desire's differentiation of its object would also eventually disappear.

This perspective, although easy to map out, is harder to implement because we live under the double law of monosexuality and of the couple. Across the political spectrum and in all social classes, except for certain libertine currents, these imperatives are followed: only make love with one of the genders, and only make love through copulation, that is, with a single person at a time.

The very idea of toppling this dictatorship can only occur to the sexually obsessed, as the bourgeoisie calls them, who are forcibly marginalized and more or less tolerated according to their social standing. But it is precisely these marginalized groups, because their powerful system of phantasy so particularizes their desire and brings about such maniacal erotic inscriptions on their body, which are pushed away from sexual polyvalence and act like antique collectors obsessing over glass vases.

In addition, today's political exacerbation of sexual insurgency arises from an excessively doctrinaire critique of foul social phallocracy and from a slightly simplistic reversal of the contentions of power, in the sense that these movements, influenced by Leftist methodology, are both overly irascible and overly ideological. It follows that these revolutionary projects have retained a multiplicity of postures of refusal fighting between themselves. Although they maintain a clear picture of their political enemies and oppressors, even amongst the so-called militants of desire, the willingness to expand desire is confronted with a radical refusal on the part of the different autonomous groups of sexual struggle, whether they be gays, lesbians or women's liberation.

They believe that the difficult pursuit of the non-differentiation of desire is politically premature, or that it is depoliticized and even tainted with mysticism. Thus a homosexual trying to allow heterosexual desire to reappear from beneath the tangle of his fears of women would be accused of treachery and assimilated to someone who, pulled in by orthodox psychoanalysis, accepts to be healed of perversion by a society to which he stands opposed. Or he would be accused of being an alibi for official sexual ideology since he would have joined it.

We are thus witness to the establishment of a series of counter-terrorisms that congeal and exclude one another. Their apparent alliance, such as the one struck up between the gays and lesbians, simply relies on different refutations of the same system. All sexual minorities thus crystallize on their particular specificity. We might think that such atomization is in fact a necessary stage, because it is useful for the margins to encircle and encroach upon normalcy in a thousand different ways. Yet the margins should not combat the margins, for this will just strengthen normalcy.

Of all the political observations that can be made about desire, the most obvious is that there is nothing more racist than desire as it has been transmitted to us, and there is nothing more discriminatory than the absolute power of desire as it continues to tunnel along single-mindedly. We need to decide if we will allow this racism to develop in our sacrosanct desire, or if revolution must also, and perhaps foremost, start with desire's struggle to expulse its own racist foundations.

I hear cries of protest already. You interrupt to tell me that wanting to desire what we do not is simply Christian charity. You exclaim that we cannot impose any work at all upon desire. On the side of the true revolution, it is our duty to speak of desire, but we do not have the right to speak of will, for that immediately evokes voluntarism and even fascism. Many revolutions prohibit voluntarism even if that volition is oriented towards the wandering of sexual flows. Our desiring machines can misfire, of course, but only beyond our consciousness or behind our backs.

The concepts of work, of will, I know what they mean in the mouths of Brezhnev or Paul VI, and more generally in mouths that can spew out morals but never take in a dick. But work also means something in terms of fermentation, of imagination and of bringing to life. And I can never really forget that voluptuousness and volition share the same etymological origin.

For a homosexual, changing life, changing his life means, first of all, that he must start trying to live his desire openly, without any exquisite guilt or veiled terror. But must we wait for capitalist society to make homosexuality licit, as it has started to do in certain countries, to escape as if by contradiction the exclusive authority of homosexuality (of one homosexuality among many) and to start prophesizing in domains that will remain prohibited or cursed once the major perversions have ceased to be minor.

Will any desire, apart from obedience, ever be able to structure itself otherwise than as transgression or counter-transgression? The broadening of desire starts today, for those who anticipate or desire it so. Limiting oneself to a sexual path, under the pretext that it is one's desire and that it corresponds to a political opportunity for deviance, strengthens the bi-polarization of the ideology of desire that has been forged by the bourgeoisie.

And please do not tell me that I am touching here upon an embryonic morality that consists in going towards women when we love men, and vice-versa. Desire must be allowed to function on any object. And not only on a body other than one's own. And not only on one body instead of two or more, simultaneously. And not only on the age class of youth or on the esthetic class of beauty, the formal elements of the class struggle. And not only on one of the two phantasmatic modalities of masochism or masochism disguised as sadism. And not only on one of the two sexes. And not only, assuming these differentiations will eventually disappear, on the human species.

Hearing this, it makes no difference if the touchy nationalists of homosexuality fear that they will lose their sexual identity; they might say this is utopia, political resignation or even a bourgeois orgy. Such an explosion of desire is not affiliated with the sham bisexuality put on by a certain libertine and hipster bourgeoisie when it engages in its cold and phallocratic lasciviousness. This path leads desiring machines towards the desire to desire and not to covetousness. It knows the urgency of the struggle against the phallus (which we must not, of course, confuse with the penis). And once desire spreads, it eludes the royalty of masculine libidinal economy, it contradicts the establishment of power based on the usage of sex, a power which is phallic in our society but which could possibly be clitoral or uterine in another.

Once homosexual desire emerges in someone's history, or in his or her environment, as *something other than a constraint or a transgression*, sex can no longer be heterosexual or homosexual unless it is stated to become reactionary. Yet this remains, perhaps, a rare occurrence. Perhaps we are underestimating repression and sexual misery. Perhaps this reflects a privileged attitude on our part, but we each must speak from where we stand.

Of course, wanting to extend the territories of sexual desire, through proliferation and wandering, calls for behaviors that are easier to adopt for gays than for lesbians. The former, by claiming to be revolutionaries, also claim to be ass fucks. The latter, on the contrary, can only be revolutionaries by negating the postulate of any male penetration and all forms of rape, real or tacit, that it entails. At present, a woman conscious of masculine oppression (even if this oppression has been incorporated into her desire) can find no form of rescue in a male, taken with all the horror the term implies, for she anticipates, senses and recognizes that she will inevitably become his prey.

What would happen if these natural allies, the gays and lesbians, although quite distant in their forms of desire, decided to make love between themselves. This strange perspective (that a logical mind would qualify as absurd) might allow us to discover whether pederasty hides the worst, most insidious cult of the phallus behind its revolt. Might it not instigate a desire for tenderness rather than for covetousness? The theory of desiring-machines, although helpful, is so fashionable that we use it to cover up the tenderness in desire. As if tenderness, like cynicism, was not a part of the machine, as active as the others and just as interconnected with the libidinal-economic system.

If we want to get to the bottom, or the dick of this, we queers will eventually have to bring our bodies closer to those of women who refuse men. To stay away from women is almost as contemptuous as to exert the sadism of the hunt or of the family fucking. This kind of behavior is a remote imitation of what heterosexuals do when they cut women out of their lives and social circles, relegating them to the false alliance of the bedroom. If we want to end the shame that men have imposed on women, and to which our fear (or sacred veneration) of them contributes, our bodies must understand the reasons for the lesbian repulsion of men, and if it arises from what we have between our legs, or from what we do with it, and what that means.

Loving boys myself, I see no other way to do this but to encounter feminine homosexuality in a place where the naked body is not more important than speech or political struggle; where the entire game of skin and muscle is not obsessed by the incoercible need for penetration; where a smile is not necessarily the flash of white on a TV screen; where a kiss is given, but not like in some country ball, for we all know where that leads.

I am not here prophesizing the good news. I am just expressing my desire, regardless of whether it is theoretical or carnal, and what difficulties it might encounter. I write down this desire, despite its contradiction, for I cannot imagine that it does not linger somewhere in other gays' minds or hidden behind a theoretical defense just like the one I have expounded. How can we gays and lesbians, through our bodies, dismantle this steam-hammer of the mutual negation of desire?

I am fed up with desire. Obsession is not what we do; it's what we don't do. I want to know what happens when I pretend not to desire. Or at least I want my desire to know it. I am tired of the officer saying: "*I don't want to know!*"

All research on desire should be research on non-desire, on what blocks desire. In the philosophy department at Vincennes where speech on desire holds sway, as it does here, I wanted to hold a day-long group investigation on non-desire that would be undertaken by people who declare they do not desire each other. Was it a ridiculous idea, a means to bury the claim to non-desire under its own absurdity? Can we even still believe in the usefulness of speaking about desire when those who speak continue to obey the prohibition of touch, as if speech and touch were absolutely separate domains?

Sometimes this situation of non-desire, for example, between gays and lesbians, seems to result from a tenacious optical illusion that any theoretical discourse, starting with mine, only reinforces. Because virility is also this desire to define and verbalize relations in order to give them meaning and usefulness. All philosophical discourse, all political and all economic discourse is discharged, instead of sperm, from men who are terrified of the opening they issue from, and to which their penis returns alone, without philosophy, without politics and without economics.

Crushed beneath the logic of man, woman is still incapable of living without him, and without his logic. Man is ancient. Woman is future. The masculine homosexual is caught between both. When he becomes feminine, it is only according to a masculine model. His only existence is the phallus. For his virile mythology, the lesbians who construct their relationships without the phallus seem like an empty mirror reflecting an empty mirror.

And yet they possess the lack he lacks. They know the operative secret of this illusion of lack; they bring us face to face with the evidence that such lack is not truly lack but that it is energy without power, the castration of castration, something we can desire and enjoy. Without them we would not ever learn anything we do not already know. They accuse us queers of reducing all homosexuality to our own form of it, they claim that we are obliterating theirs, that we are a collection of dicks, that we transmit the eternal phallic discourse they find even more toxic in those who have decided to become castrated men rather than women.

Yes, I can only think of homosexuality as a male. Yes, I refuse to speak of feminine homosexuality that I do not understand and of which I could only produce a fatally masculine theory. And all queers can say the same. This is why the FHAR sank beneath the weight of the phallus. This is why the FHAR felt it necessary to vent its bile upon male society, speaking to the authority to which it naturally belonged. This is why the lesbians fled.

I now dream of lesbians who do not copy men, who live without the phallus and without the terror of the phallus. Even if one single lesbian exists, I wish to lie at her side, like someone on the point of fainting, like a future woman. For an instant, for the instant of the sexual revolution, I will think of myself as a lesbian.

Oh! Wanting to be woman, to be fertile, to be cunt-ile, rather than feeling the capitalist desire to impregnate! I know I am ranting. Long live snails! What luck they have to be both male and female without ever copying the other gender. I proclaim the end of ostriches that keep their head in the sand and refuse to see that the revolutionary explosion of sexuality and the means to blow it apart lie in that difficult articulation of feminine and masculine homosexuality. What is this revolutionary hell where the men and women fighting phallocracy do not have any right to the sensuality they might share among themselves?

I would like to go, stupidly, towards the bodies that my anxiety has kept me from. It makes no difference if I do it, or if it is someone else; as long as a man who thinks he loves men approaches a woman who thinks she loves women. I imagine this move can only come from men. They are the ones guiltier of tyranny, both in feeling and in reality. But it should be a fag. Women, whether they are right about this or not, feel he is less of an oppressor than other men. And it should be a man with a dick, because the question is not to cut it off, but to invent a new way of using it.

Should we wait for society to change, for the male spirit to disappear? The pederast seems to be, among all phallus carriers, the one who is the least suspect of phallocracy. I would like to know if this is true. Can his body show a lesbian the phallus? Can a lesbian accept this approach without being passive or tensing up, if that is where her issue with fags comes up; namely, that they have dissolved in their sexual plumbing what she calls love without fear of ridicule. Like two virgins, can they play together and enact the childhood of bodies? And can this make them come, since resuscitating courtly love is out of the question?

Even if male hypocrisy was to burst forth, and perhaps it is already in these lines, things would at least be clear. We'd know that the male had advanced smooth-tongued, hiding his desire for power. We'd know it is utopian to want love untainted by deceitful relations of power. We'd know it's all a booby-trap. We'd know that what ferments history has accumulated in our desire prohibit anything religious there, by which we mean religion in the epistemological sense, the sense it had before it was tainted by the clerical religions or the political religions that have taken its place. We'd know that an offering, again in the epistemological sense of the word, is a calculated move, the form of a spirit of conquest, a masochistic avatar or God knows what psychoanalysis or dialectics will be happy to discover there.

If, on the contrary, in the embryonic couple formed by a fag and a lesbian, the woman could feel —extravagantly or miraculously, by itself or among other complex movements—the *welcoming* of a male body that is forgetting its gender, and if she persisted in her refusal, then we could no longer attribute a political alibi drawn from the situation of the social body to this retreat.

Suddenly, I feel my attempt to describe this couple has gone too far, that its experience can't escape being theoretical, tinged with Machiavellianism and terribly experimental. And then I laugh and I don't give a fuck. I know the time will come when the desire to desire shall be stronger than the desire to dissect. In a month, in a year, what difference does it make? Whether it happens to me or to someone else, I know it will happen. I know that hands and mouths arouse penises or clitorises. Must they necessarily belong to the same gender as ours, under the pretense that all policing enforces their belonging to the other?

The ruling classes are the ones who have split and mutilated desire. The bourgeoisie invented the notion of homosexuality and made it into a ghetto. We must not forget this. There are two sexes on earth, but this is only to hide the fact that there are three, four, ten, thousands, once you throw that old hag of the idea of nature overboard. There are two sexes on earth but only one sexual desire.

9

*And what if analysis and desire finally sided. What if it
was desire that finally led analysis?*

— Gilles Deleuze

No statement should be pronounced if it aims at
hiding the specific constellation of the speaker's daily
life. The customs of writing, however, lead to the sep-
aration of theory and confession, criticism and avowal, political criticism and personal discernment, as if
mixing genres were preposterous. Yet there comes a
time when I wonder if my research on homosexuality,
combined with the explorations of other homosexuals
with whom I share the need to transform life, can
coexist with my silence on our profound differences
in daily life. By this I mean the differences that might
lead them to consider me either privileged or disloyal.
Whether I asked for it or not, what happened to me
didn't happen to anyone else that was involved in the
same struggle. It's lucky I'm gay, because I give a bad
impression at the FHAR. As gay as I am, I've been with
the same man for eighteen years. (You can't say I've

got the right ticket for the revolution!) All those who see the reactionary specter of marriage in the institution of coupledom, no matter how it functions and how open it is, all those who devote most of their energy to only participating in short-lived couplings, might be terrified of this. But how could I speak of gays and of the revolution without this preliminary avowal? Of course, I can only say it without any self-justification, without defending myself, without considering this particular avatar of homosexuality to be the necessary path to follow. This is difficult to believe in the crazy post-Leftist environment, where no one forgives, and where friendships are more aggressive than they are generous, helpful or accommodating.

I sometimes lose the possibility of discerning, among the behaviors that surround me, between revolutionary effort and the conscious or unconscious recitation of the bourgeoisie, for it is hard to tell where someone has come from and how trying or easy was the distance traveled. In any case, one cannot deny the terrorism inflicted by the young on those who are no longer young, or the mute or vindictive blame that those who are not yet in the grips of the economic machine impose upon anyone who occupies a place there, whether that place is voluntary or not. One cannot deny the example of urban nomadism and refusal of constraints that the fringes of one generation sets for all the others, even if they pay the price for it by standing accused of being parasites.

All revolutionaries will have to become parasites of society, and more and more irresponsibly at that, or they will still be the knights of some morality or another. Our energy is devoted to the destruction of the animal that feeds us, and this remains true for those of us who inevitably feed it in return.

But let me return to desire, to my own and to the geography in which it is inscribed. As part of a long lasting homosexual couple, I am struck by the obvious fact that this has only been allowed for certain marginal bourgeois, more or less called artists, whose perversion is sanctioned by the environing liberal bourgeoisie in exchange for a production that is supposed to entertain, educate and enrich, for it is the bourgeoisie who exploit and provide the circulation of this production in the end. Those are my relations with the system. But what are my relations with homosexuals?

A couple is something homosexuals do not like, something they almost never like; it is even what they hate or fear the most. The machine constructed for homosexuals by heterosexual society (and sometimes used by libertines) is an anti-couple cruising machine. Under the guise of perpetual drift and sway, it is a strange machine that nonetheless displays strong analogies with capitalist accumulation, in that it continuously projects into the past, due to its mechanism of collection and seriality, just as it projects into the future due to its forward-looking mechanism through which the conqueror thinks of his next conquest immediately upon completing the first.

One can, of course, only retain of this machine its disjunctive and profoundly subversive action towards legitimate union and official fidelity. But it did not initially function according to that goal. It does not attack anything; it protects itself from a peril. If cruising plays leapfrog while conjugality plays kitty corner and house, they both originate in the same anxiety about solitude.

I know this cruising machine quite well. Or rather, it has known me well enough that I can verify that couples disrupt it. Cruising is best done alone. Capitalism might easily say this machine constitutes the sad destiny of gay people, without mentioning that it created this destiny itself: the couple or the troll, the choice is yours, it's just like work or vagrancy. Have we let ourselves be imprisoned by this, and do we recite the terror of the couple as badly as married couples recite the terror of polygamy? Is it possible that we desire coupledom just as secretly as the bourgeois desire to be Casanovas?

In this case, under the pretext that the building and the perpetuating of love is bewitched by marriage, we supposedly fear it in a panic, and thus reproduce a reversed form of the conditions in which masculine bourgeoisie represses the love that rises and consumes itself immediately. In sum, what phallocrats ridiculously, and in a nostalgic manner, call "to be free," in the misleading margins of the 5 to 7 where they construct assembly-line adultery... this freedom from the rope around the neck they have imposed upon themselves (which by the force of habit becomes just another robe around the neck)... in sum, the Casanova-type dream of the normals would be a gay person's reality, running around chasing a hundred million beautiful boys, beautiful cocks or beautiful asses, exhausting his strength and time in finding them, seducing them, and naturally, leaving them. If only the straying ass and the nomadic cock were everywhere! But in homosexuals, such tourists are very conventional and can only withstand a limited number of climates.

There is, in this desire to crystallize nothing, in this desire not to allow any object of desire to last, something at once marvelous and despairing if you do not have the vocation for solitude. Something marvelous for it is the state of algae drifting in the ocean. Something despairing for the rule is not to go farther than the first ejaculation with anyone, and not to let any part of the known into the unknown. It is quite telling that the FHAR boys confess they can't make love among themselves once they start knowing one another, once they become friends. Isn't this falling back into the prohibition against sexual relations between same-sex militants and political comrades which the FHAR took upon itself to combat? And anyway, isn't it absurd to claim to know someone who has not come thanks to us, that we have not yet seen come, someone that we are hastening to leave and with which we refuse to share anything once we ejaculate?

The cruising machine has thus established an impenetrable border between what turns us on and what makes us think. This border is perhaps a defense mechanism against the intrusion of relations of power. Perhaps it is also a romantic resurgence of the desire to love what can only occur once. I cannot but see in it as well the instinctive fear of the death of desire that we know to be inscribed in marriage, if not a fear of death itself. (But the philosophers of the sexual revolution are not concerned with the relations of desire to death: they leave this to the Oriental mystics.) Constructed like capitalism against death, the cruising machine carries death within it just like capitalism, for instead of being madly in love with what is present, it desires what is absent, it always desires the next object, it constructs itself on the establishment and sacred assumption of lack, according to the absolute criteria of consumption.

If I leave my house to enjoy the weather, the street or the night, to buy bread or go see a friend, and if I come upon a boy that I like, gay or not, I am blissfully enjoying the present. But if I leave my house every night to find another queer by cruising the places where other queers hang around, I am nothing but a proletarian of my desire who no longer enjoys the air or the earth and whose masochism is reduced to an assembly line. In my entire life, I have only ever really met what I was not trying to seduce.

Clearly, homosexual flirtatiousness represents a formidable power of disjunction, constantly at work and extremely efficient as a nuptial deconstructor. But how can we deny that it issues from a cult of frustration that padlocks itself? Of course, I have as many criticisms to level against the homosexual couple that has decided to settle down, against its fallacious security and against the erotic subterfuges of triangulation or groupings with which it perversely attempts to attract one or several external bodies (and these criticisms are all autocritiques).

In any case, that gay couple, whether in wedlock or seriously engaged, is clearly felt by the cruising machine to be the bourgeois grain of sand gripping the homosexual chase. A grain of sand that is forbidden and that leaves the cruiser dumbfounded.

If this couple is closed, with all that the long assimilation of the purely economic mechanism of jealousy implies, the cruisers shall drag it through the mud. In any case, bourgeois ideology has contrived to pin on old homosexual couples the clichés we all know: wrinkled, petrified, without offspring, submerged in useless confrontation and imprisoned in the law of the mirror, they perfectly reproduce the defects of the bourgeois family without even the solution of projecting onto their children. Since they have been impressed by the cruising machine early on, as are all homosexuals, it sometimes happens that their reciprocal code allows them to return to it when the asphyxiation grows too strong, but it is then too late and its treachery is too evident to allow them to find anything in the cruise other than a more bitter isolation. These are the disaster victims of homosexuality, artificially reterritorialized in the apparatus that their desire could have been able to dissolve.

The way the FHAR rejected some of these couples was a sight to see. It operated through an underhanded process of non-recognition when the couples spontaneously showed up thinking their homosexuality was a sufficient passport for admission. No one sought to discover why, or how, they hadn't found another issue to the deadlock they were in, or to ask what trap they had fallen into. Age racism ran at full capacity, as if the revolution could only be made by the young generation and by censuring everything that was over thirty. (Age racism was just as strong as the racism of beauty, for the same thing happened to those crying for help from the boondocks. The FHAR responded only if it was a young and beautiful body asking for help.)

What if, on the contrary, that gay couple is an open couple? It can be immediately objected that pigs can't fly, that a couple that has settled down has, by that token, become closed and gentrified. It is true that, in any case, the couple shall be perceived by bachelor gays on the prowl as an ambiguous object of desire, conceivable only if cut in half. And it shall be decided, as a security measure, that this couple refuses to be cut in half and that it cannot be open unless it spontaneously decides to break up. For the most rigid law of our sexual and emotional ideology, affecting both homosexuals and heterosexuals, does not concern the shape or sex of the desired object but its number: it is dangerous and thus prohibited to desire several people at the same time, and even more so if those people desire one another.

The jealous couple, the couple of owners, where each partner owns the other's body, is in the end pretty reassuring. The gang can get the better of it. Or one can get around it by choosing one of the two partners, who might be extremely pleased. But imagine a couple ready to share with others the matching of complementary or separate desires that it has formed, destroyed, reconstructed through lengthy patience. Imagine two subjects ready to extend without hypocrisy the bastard alliance of their reciprocal powers as well as the critique of these powers. (If I ask that this couple be imagined, it is because I am certain neither of its real existence nor of seeing an image of my own couple reflected there.)

Look at those two boys seemingly exposing themselves to all exterior irruptions, perhaps at the risk of destroying their intimate cell or even unconsciously desiring its explosion, yet who believe it still has energy to give. Look at that glorious and equivocal couple of hustlers who built a fire and own a hearth and yet caress you with their eyes with as much desire as that with which they observe themselves. A truly moving sight.

It is so difficult to experience the number three in the equilibrium of desires without three becoming the number two plus one. Someone is always shut out or becomes entrenched, and there he goes asking for a little bit of coupledom, there he is on the point of asking one of the two others to choose between himself and the third. Falling under the spell of the couple is not inscribed in human nature, as the priests of idealism and dialectic materialism will claim. On the contrary, it is an intrigue of the *socius*, and its most insane invention to date. I believe neither the cruising nor the wedding machine can combat it.

The wedding machine is loath to confront the couple with situations that overpower it unless it is trying to break it and immediately crystallize a new couple that is just as privileged. And yet, I do not know if a couple is bourgeois according to the definition its duration affords. Is a lasting couple an ivory tower? This is a question to which I myself, living with a man, have never found an answer. It is a question to which I shall have neither the bad conscience to answer "yes," nor the nerve to answer "no." Rather, I have the impression we are all in prison, whether we find refuge in couples or whether we flee them like the plague.

Cruising machine or wedding machine, in fact, these are probably two models made by the same coupling industry. For they always produce a couple that we then try to no avail to break down, either perpetually renewing it once our balls are empty or exposing it to the storms of an external desire. And the worst of it is, between those two machines, between the quick fuck and sexual property, between indulging the senses and making sense, we have wiped the slate clean.

If we want the revolution to penetrate desire, if we want desire to engender its own revolution, we must figure out where the law of the couple is the strongest and where libidinal energy is the most conservative. Is it in the man who carries his couple with him to all his adventures, or is it in the couple carrying itself from adventure to adventure? And we must also figure out in which case the couple has greater chances of exploding. The only positive sign will occur where we find the greatest number of multiple and simultaneous connections for desire, with no preferential investment.

The most vigorous weapon against the couple is the permanent desire to desire. It must, of course, extend way beyond those structures known or unknown to sexual desire, and it must also have curbed the desire to be desired, which supposes that we start by desiring ourselves well. The desire to desire and to be desired, that's love, finally wrenched from the fetor of bourgeois humanism as well as from the childishness of mystical liturgies. My weakness is not to believe in it, like a believer, but to see in it like a seer my desire as it ceases to repeat itself. What joy when I intercept it in its movements, just as it switches between machines! The desire that says "*Why not?*" rather than "*No.*" The desire that shoots its refusals one by one. The phoenix of desire, snatched away from avarice and usury, finally engaged in polymorphous expenditure, in seepage, in prodigality, in dilapidation.

10

The body never believed in progress. Its religion is not the future but the today.

— Octavio Paz

Trying to take power is a dead-end. Trying to destroy power is an even greater lure, especially if we neglect to shake off this very particular form of power called self-domination. How can we destroy the operative or imaginary power that the other weighs down upon us without arming ourselves with power through exercising strength over ourselves? And if power only begins in the presence of two people, how can we exert strength over ourselves without this eventually becoming a power that splashes others with its silence, its indifference, and its tranquility?

There is no worse power, no more magical-sounding power, than that wielded by those who pretend to refuse it even as they remain beings of power, albeit in isolation. There is no worse, more insoluble contradiction for a social being than to want to destroy power, that den of snakes, each eating each other's tail, that place where we are each the biter and the bit. As long as some sort of capacity remains, as long as there is some potentiality, a basic energetic faculty, power is at the doorstep. We stand condemned to power as long as this society of competition surrounding and impregnating us remains as it is; that is, as long as equality of strength or weakness is but an illusion or a brief miracle. That equality is the utopian state of homosexual homosexuality, where all relations of power are leveled and where desire resembles a mathematical identity between two numbers.

Power endures on the ruins of obligation. With the revolutionary machine on its way, the golden calf could say: "*My power is to emit a golden brilliance, not to distribute power.*" To propel the revolutionary machine, we must not act like surveyors who consider the problem solved.

Power is not something to be destroyed: that remains beyond our means. What we can do, however, is understand its mechanism and do everything possible to disrupt it. Whether we do this by overriding power instead of censuring it, by working towards the generalized confusion of powers, by driving the rules of the game over the edge, we must always remember that these activities will continue to be exercises of power, nocturnal perhaps, but not the desired emergence of weakness between all men. Besides, at this point, it would be best if the senses could rip power away from sense. Then, we would only speak wails and cries, laughter and dancing, noise and music.

Both for dialectical materialism and for psychoanalysis, the material is the non-body. All struggles for the return of the body have been so contaminated by the non-body that when they speak of the body they only accentuate its exile. We forget that the content of speech is only the container of our universe.

"*The power of words or the moving of skins*," writes the most well known poet in France today. Intelligent or incomprehensible words speak of skins, but skins continue to obey an inexplicable tyranny, one that is considered sacred in that it is called desire and draws its energy from the abysses of the unconscious. Desire has become God but has remained blind and mechanical, true to its construction by the capitalist apparatus and family history.

When shall we be able to shatter the power of words by the movement of skins? We shall not count and index all those old domestic machines that have domesticated desire: sewing machines of desire, freezers of desire, brake presses of desire, paper cutters, riveters, grinding machines and plows of desire, irons of desire, routers and rolling-mills. They are all rattling and hissing inside until we end up crying: "*I am free! I only desire what I like!*" What I like, myself, is to desire all bodies that can produce joy and revolution.

11

Freud and Marx aren't bad, but we prefer motorcycles.
— *The Bulletin of Aubervilliers Youth,*
Number 2, October 1972

Whom am I speaking to here? To all those who speak of revolution without doing it, that is to say, also to myself. My discourse is, of course, phallic, and even more so as it relies on clear and ancient grammar. Aside from brief hysterical cracklings followed by formidable silences, all writing is rubbish, Artaud told us so, and saying it, he added his own turd to thousands of others.

Can madness appear in writing? Can writing be a kind of madness if madness is the negation of all order? Writing that communicates (and that becomes a commodity) gets as close to madness as it can without ever entering into it for fear of ceasing to communicate.

For madness to be transmitted, it must be put to reason, that is, put in prison. The one who fails to do so finds him/herself alone in the world, locked down in his cell. The one who succeeds is already an ideologue helping himself to madness, to the great plenary anxiety in which words are no longer at home. He is a cop, and a cop that doubles as a transvestite. His thinking is wearing garters concealed beneath the pants of his uniform. Such are all males discoursing on desire. That is how they frenzy and overstep, safe behind that discourse. For there is no practice in the West that is not preceded by discourse. I am one of those cops, and those garters really turn me on. And yet I dream of the day when we will no longer need fetishes.

12

Can you remind me what this is about? No use trying to fool me, I've got a good memory, I'd know right away. What was I saying?

— Roland Dubillard

Alone in his forest dwelling, an ogre had spent years building machines to force his visitors to make love to one another: machines with pulleys, chains, clocks, collars, leather leggings, metal breastplates, oscillatory, pendular, or rotating dildos. One day, some adolescents who had lost their way, seven or eight brothers, entered the ogre's house.

No one knows if the traps closed in upon them, or if the boys' curiosity was such that they closed them themselves. In any case, embedded into one another, two by two, and condemned to ejaculate until the end of time, they became the machinery of a factory without electricity and the slaves of a corpse. For they did not know that the ogre, in his attic, was dead.

semiotext(e) intervention series
